Mountain of Fire and Miracles Ministries
International Headquarters,
Lagos, Nigeria.

DELIVERANCE THROUGH THE WATCHES FOR HEALING

A PROGRAMME
THAT RUNS THROUGHOUT A WHOLE DAY
AT 3 HOUR INTERVALS

The Prayer Watches are as follows:
1st - 6am | 2nd - 9am | 3rd - 12 noon
4th - 3pm | 5th - 6pm | 6th - 9pm | 7th - 12am

This gives a total of
7 Prayer Watches.

DELIVERANCE
THROUGH THE WATCHES
FOR HEALING

ISBN 978-978-8424-81-9
Reprinted: January 2013

Published by:

Mountain of Fire and Miracles Ministries Press
13, Olasimbo Street, Onike, Yaba, Lagos.

I salute my wonderful wife, Pastor Shade, for her invaluable support in the ministry.
I appreciate her unquantifiable support in the book ministry as the cover designer, art editor and art advisor

All Scripture quotation is from the King James Version of the Bible

HEARING FROM GOD

BIBLE STUDY 1

HEARING FROM GOD

A HOW GOD COMMUNICATES

God communicates with us and reveals Himself to us:

THROUGH REVELATION: (Psalm 19:1; Isa. 40:26; Rom. 1:19-20; 2:15. Revelation the uncovering or unveiling of information.

THROUGH INSPIRATION: That is, when the Holy Spirit acts on man to make known God's revelation (Job 32:8).

THROUGH ILLUMINATION: This is a ministry of the Holy Spirit which enables those of us who are in right standing with God to understand revelations, as they pertain to our individual lives.

B HOW DO WE KNOW THE VOICE OF GOD?

To know the voice of God, we must

1. Commit our lives completely to the Lord.

2. Learn to test our impressions.
3. Be honest with ourselves and have faith.
4. Let God have access to every area of our lives.
5. Pray to God to open our faculties to receive His messages.

C WHEN GOD SPEAKS TO YOU,

1. It will glorify His name.
2. It will cause you to worship Him.
3. It will agree with the Scriptures.
4. It will impart His knowledge to you.
5. It will cause you to love others and Him more.
6. It can produce a response to God in prayer, praise, thanksgiving, worship or confessions.

D VEHICLES OF DIVINE COMMUNICATIONS:

1. Face to face in a two-way communication (Gen. 3:9; Exod. 33:11).
2. By a voice (Num. 11:17; Exod. 3:2-4; 1 Sam. 3:4).
3. By dreams (Gen. 20:6; Matt. 1:20; Acts 2:17).
4. By open visions (Acts 10:1-6; 12:7-11).
5. By closed visions (Acts 16:9:18:9-10).
6. By trance (Acts 10:9-16).
7. By angels (Luke 1:11-20, 27-28; Acts 8:26-29; Gen. 16:7; 19:1).

8. By writings, e.g., commandments on stone tablets, sentences written on the wall (Exod. 20; Dan. 5:5).
9. By miracles (Exod. 14:21; 7: 7-11; 2 Kings 5:1-17)
10. Through the written Word (The Gospels).
11. Reference to Bible passages.
12. Anointed messages and teachings.
13. Anointed counsellings.
14. Walking with holy men and women (Prov. 13:20).
15. Anointed music (2 Kings 3:15).
16. Anointed meditations.

17. Conscience.
18. Burdens of the heart.
19. Divine ideas.
20. Intuition (knowing signals).
21. Internal understanding.
22. Impression on the heart.
23. Inward witness.
24. Inner voice.
25. Outer voice (Acts 9:4-9).
26. Closed outer voice (1 Sam. 3:3-10).
27. Still small voice (1 Kings 19:12).
28. Sudden impulse.
29. Favourable and positive circumstances (Gen. 24:15-48).
30. Difficult circumstances (Deut. 8).
31. Words of wisdom.
32. Words of knowledge.
33. Faith.
34. Healing.
35. Working of miracles.
36. Prophecy.
37. Discerning of spirits.
38. Diverse kinds of tongues.

39. Interpretation of tongues.
40. Remembering the truth.
41. Intercession from within.
42. Conclusive evidence (by their fruits).
43. Divine visitation.
44. Symbolic actions (Jer. 18).

E POWER PRINCIPLES OF HEARING FROM GOD:

1. Salvation (John 10:3-4).
2. Brokenness (John 12:24).
3. Receptivity (Rev. 3:20; John 8:43; Matt. 17:5).
4. Faith (John 10:3,27; Heb. 11:6; 4:2; Rom. 10:17).
5. Attentiveness (1 Sam. 3:1-11; Exod. 3:4).
6. Discernment (John 12:26-29; 1 Kings 19:11-13).
7. Obedience.

F WHY GOD SPEAKS

1. To warn you of an impending danger - Acts 27:10.
2. To give you the picture of your destiny- Gen. 37:5-10.
3. To reveal the secrets of your enemy - 2 Kings 6:15-17.
4. To correct you - Job 5:17.
5. To carry out an assignment for Him - Jonah 1:1-2.
6. To intercede for others - Ezek. 22:30.

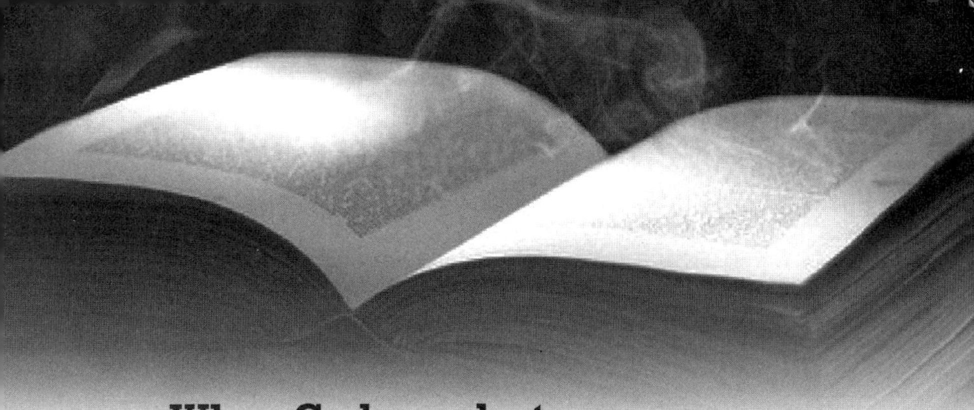

When God speaks to you. . .

...It will agree with Scriptures.

7. To work for Him - Acts 26:16-18.
8. To give you a piece of information - 1 Sam. 3:4-13.
9. To show that He loves you - Gen. 18:17-23.
10. To ask you a question- Gen. 3:9.
11. To mete out a punishment - Dan. 4:3-32.
12. To prosper you - Deut. 28:1-3.
13. To deliver you from your problems - Acts 12:7.
14. To teach you certain lessons - Exod. 24:12.
15. To create things - Gen. 1:3-31.
16. To reveal the past to you - Moses (The book of Genesis).
17. To reveal the present to you - (Gen. 19:27-28).
18. To reveal the future to you- John (Rev. 1:1-20).
19. To approve certain things - Luke 9:35.
20. To bless you - Gen. 32:26-30.
21. To caution you - 2 Sam. 12:7-11.
22. To provide for your needs - 1 Kg. 17:2-4.

23. To heal you - John 5:5-9.
24. To have a covenant with you - Gen. 15:18.
25. To anoint you - Luke 4:18.
26. To take you from darkness to light - Acts 9:4-6.

G ADVANTAGES OF HEARING FROM GOD:

1. Joy in your heart.
2. Proof that you are a privileged/ peculiar person.
3. Satan fears you.
4. Your life becomes organised.
5. Your prosperity is guaranteed.
6. You will not move with unprofitable people.
7. Makes you have a peace of mind.
8. Respect from people.
9. You will receive the blue-print of your life.
10. You will know the secrets of God and man.
11. You will become spiritually sound.

H HOW GOD SPEAKS

1. Face to face in a two-way communication - Here, God talks with you directly and you reply Him immediately in an open conversation. He talked to Adam and Eve and they replied (Gen. 3:8-19). He with Abraham and he replied (Gen. 18:17,23-33). Moses and God had a discussion (Exod. 3:4-22; 31:18).

2. ***The written Word/Bible*** - 2 Tim. 3:16: "All scripture is given by inspiration of God, and is profitable for doctrine, for reproof, for correction, for instruction in righteousness:" The Bible is the Word and voice of God. As we read it, the Lord is talking with us.

3. ***Reference to passages*** - When someone or the Holy Spirit refers you to Bible passages. Jesus referred satan to certain Bible passages (Luke 4:4,8,12).

4. ***Anointed messages/teachings*** - The sermons of an anointed minister and the teachings of an anointed teacher convey the mind of God (1Cor. 1:17-18; Acts 26:28).

5. ***Anointed counsellings*** - As an anointed counsellor counsels you, you are listening to God (as Jethro counsels Moses - Exod. 18:14-23).

6. ***Jumpy Bible verses*** - When a particular Scripture magnetises your spirit and you begin to meditate on it, God is talking with you directly (Acts 8:26-39)

7. ***Walking with holy men or women*** - The lifestyle of a holy man speaks the voice of God. The life of Abraham prospered Lot; the life of Moses prospered Joshua; the life of Paul prospered Timothy.

THOSE WHO RECOGNISED THE VOICE OF GOD:

1. The ground (Numbers 16:27-32).
2. Animals - e.g. the snake (Gen. 3:14),
   the bear - (2Kings 2:24).
3. Trees (Mark 11:20-22).
4. The dead (John 11:43-44.)
5. Demons (Matt. 8:28-32).
6. Light (Gen. 1:3).
7. Water (2 Kings 2:21-22).
8. Winds (Matt. 8:23-27).
9. Mountains (Matt. 21:21).
10. Diseases and sicknesses (Mark 1:40-42).
11. Infirmity (Luke 13:11-13).
12. Rivers, hills, valleys and forests (Ezek. 6:1-3).
13. Food - Mark 6:38-43.
14. Cooking pot and bottle of oil (1 Kings 17:14-16).

THE WORD OF GOD CAME TO THE FOLLOWING:

1. Abraham (Gen. 15:1).
2. Moses (Exod. 3:4-10).
3. Joshua (Jos. 1:1-7).
4. Balaam (Num. 22:38).
5. Samuel (1 Sam. 3:4-14).
6. Solomon (1 Kings 3:5-6).
7. David (2 Sam. 2:1).

8. Shemaiah (1 Kings 12:22).

9. The young prophet (1 Kings 13:1).

10. Elijah (1 Kings 17:24).

11. Jonah (Jonah 1:1-2).

12. Nathan (1 Chro. 17:3-4).

13. Isaiah (Isa. 7:3).

14. Jeremiah (Jer. 43:1).

15. Ezekiel (Ezek. 25:1-3).

16. The Israelites in the wilderness (Acts 10:36; Exod. 19:9).

17. John the Baptist (Luke 3:2).

18. Peter (Luke 5:1-4).19. The Apostles of Christ (Acts 6:7).

20. The Samaritans (Acts 8:14).

21. The Gentiles in Judea (Acts 11:1).

22. Sergius Paulus (Acts 13:7).

23. The Thessalonians (1 Thess. 2:13).

24. The whole world (Matt. 3:17).

WHAT ARE FALSE VOICES?

1. Voices that mislead or seduce (Gen. 3:1-10).

2. Voice of temptation (Matt. 4:10).

3. Voices of evil spirits confessing the truth (Act.16:17).

4. Voices of false prophets or prophets that God did not send (Jer 28:12-17, 14:15).
5. The voice of self (Gal. 6:3-4).
6. Voice of prophets speaking from own hearts (Jer. 14:14-15,1 Kg. 13:11-29).
7. Voices of prophets speaking what the people want to hear (Isaiah 30:10).
8. Voices of commercial prophets or those hungry for gain (Acts 8:9-23).
9. Voices of prophets under the influence of lying Spirits (1 Kings 22:1-23).
10. Voices of miserable comforters who judge and condemn instead of encouraging.
11. Voices of mockery like those of Michal, Sambalat and Tobia (2 Sam. 6:20, Neh. 6:12).
12. Voices of the oppressors and persecutors, like Goliath for example (1 Sam. 17:1-23).
13 The voice of ignorance (Matt. 12:22-24).
14. Voices of flatterers or soothsayers and hero worshippers (Prov. 26:28, 29:5, 20:19). 126:8-9).
21. False doctrines or doctrines of the devil (1 Tim. 4:1).
22. False voices are generally an instrument of satan to counter the voice of God in a man's life. The Proverbs calls it an enticing words of familiar friends (Prov. 1:10). The good Shepherd leads us through His word and Spirit, but the false voices are fashioned tolead against the words of eternal life or cause men to look back

CHARACTERISTICS AND SIGNS OF FALSE VOICES:

1. Deceptive, being deceived or self deceiving (Act 13:10, Jer. 9:6).
2. Leads to confusion, uncertainty, worry, irritation, anger and condemnation (Job. 22:1-5).
3. Feeling of rejection and fear, even after a divine encounter (1 Kings 19:1-18).
4. Slippery success, renewed aggression or evil trade by barter.
5. Frustration, endless pursuit, perpetual and incurable spiritual illness (James 4:3, Jer. 15:15).
6. Spiritual and physical backwardness (Jer. 7:24).
7. Promises and high hopes that fail (Jer. 8:15).

What kind of voice is leading your life? If your experience in life cannot match the Word of God or your experience in life is making you lose hope in Him who created you and died for you, then clear your ears, you may be hearing the wrong voice.

AGENTS AND SOURCES OF FALSE VOICES

1. Satan, his workers or agents and his victims (Mat. 4:1-10, 1 Sam. 28:1-8).
2. The world or the corporate man and his inventions (Rom. 12:2).

3. The flesh through its indispensable appetites, feelings and reactions (Gal.5:19-21).
4. The individual man and his imagination (Jer. 7:24).

THE ARMOUR AGAINST FALSE VOICES

1. You must be dead to sin, the world and the flesh, and be alive to God through Jesus Christ (Rm 6:1-11).
2. You must be filled with the Holy Spirit, not just attending a firebrand church. There is no corporate anointing for salvation (Acts 2:38).
3. Do not be delivered to do abomination (Jer. 7:8-11).
4. Hunger and thirst after righteousness through the Word of God (Mat. 5:6).
5. Pray and fast in hope of eternal life through our Lord Jesus Christ (Rm. 2:7).
6. Be addicted to obedience, even when it hurts (1 Sam. 15:22).
7. Put on the whole armour of God. (Eph. 6:11-18).

If you have the Holy Spirit on the inside, you can stand any kind of battle on the outside

THE HOLY SPIRIT?

WHO IS THE HOLY SPIRIT?

MEMORY VERSE:

Zech. 4:6: "Then he answered and spake unto me, saying, This is the word of the Lord unto Zerubbabel, saying, Not by might, nor by power, but by my spirit, saith the Lord of Hosts

TEXT: Acts 2

INTRODUCTION These series of studies are going to be some of the most important Bible studies you have ever had. This is because of the importance of the Holy Spirit in the life of the believer. There is a lot of ignorance amongst believers regarding the personality, the activities and the role of the Holy Spirit in the life of a Christian. When thoroughly understood in the context of these teachings, the spiritual poverty will be eliminated forever.

IMPORTANT TRUTHS ABOUT THE HOLY SPIRIT

1. The Christian's heart is the Holy Spirit's home.
2. Unless we have within us that which is above us, we soon shall yield to the pressures around us.
3. If you have the Holy Spirit on the inside, you can withstand any kind of battle on the outside.
4. Christ departed, so that the Holy Spirit could be imparted.
5. The human spirit fails, unless the Holy Spirit fills.
6. You cannot drink of the Holy Spirit on Sunday and the spirits of the world during the week.
7. The Holy Spirit can do more in a minute than what we can do for ourselves in a lifetime.
8. He, who has the Holy Spirit in his heart and the Scripture in his hands, has all he needs.
9. The Holy Spirit is God at work.

10. To build temples is easier than to be temples of the Holy Spirit.
11. One taught by the Spirit knows the will of God.

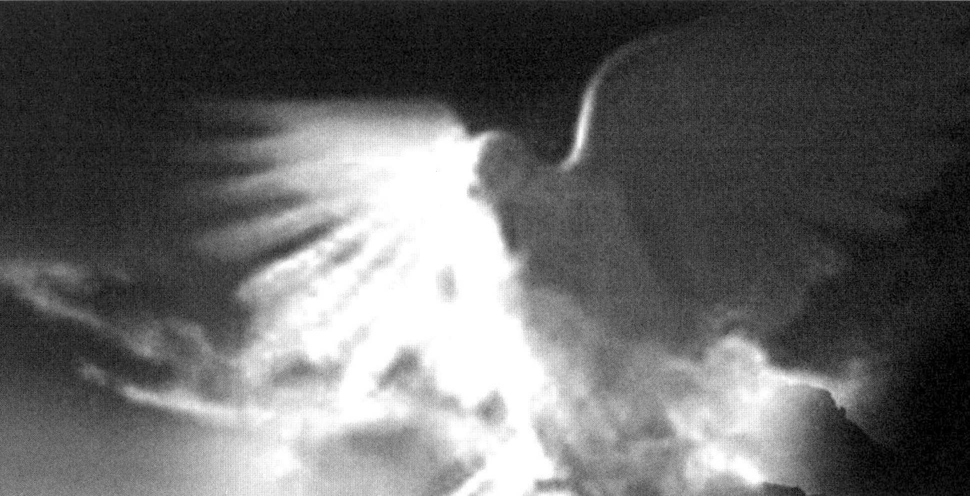

12. Without the Holy Spirit, the preacher is as helpless before a sinner needing a Saviour, as Samson before Delilah.

WHO IS THE HOLY SPIRIT?

1. Holy Spirit is the executor of the Trinity.
2. The Holy Spirit is God's executive agent in the world today.
3. The Holy Spirit is the bridge to God within you.
4. The Holy Spirit is the voice of God instilled within His children.
5. The Holy Spirit is the constant resource and companion.

6. The Holy Spirit is God.
7. The Holy Spirit is a Person with a mind, emotions and will.
8. The Holy Spirit is God present with us and active amongst us.
9. The Holy Spirit is God around us in everyday experience.
10. The Holy Spirit is part of the Trinity, whom Jesus promised would come to be our Counsellor (John 14:6).
11. The Holy Spirit is the Spirit of the Father.
12. The Holy Spirit is the Spirit of Jesus Christ.
13. The Holy Spirit is the Creator and Giver of life (Job 33:4).
14. The Holy Spirit is the director of ministers (Acts 8:29; 16:6,7).
15. The Holy Spirit is the instructor of ministers (1 Cor. 2:13).
16. The Holy Spirit is the one who speaks in and by the prophets (Acts 1:16).
17. The Holy Spirit is the one who strives with sinners (Gen. 6:3).
18. The Holy Spirit is the one who reproves (John 16:8).
19. The Holy Spirit is the Comforter (Acts 9:31).
20. The Holy Spirit is the helper of our infirmities (Rom. 8:26).
21. The Holy Spirit is the teacher (John 14:26; 1 Cor. 12:3).

22. The Holy Spirit is the one who guides (John 16:13).
23. The Holy Spirit is the one who sanctifies (Rom. 15:16).
24. The Holy Spirit is the one who testifies of Christ (John 15:26).
25. The Holy Spirit is the one who glorifies Christ (John 16:14).
26. The Holy Spirit is the one who searches all things (Rom. 11:33).
27. The Holy Spirit is the one who dwells with the saints (John 14:17).
28. The Holy Spirit is the one who inspires the writing of the Scriptures (2 Sam. 23:2).

29. The Holy Spirit is the one present at work in creation (Gen. 1:2).
30. The Holy Spirit is the one who came upon Joseph in (Gen. 41:38).
31. The Holy Spirit is the one who came upon Moses in (Num. 11:17).
32. The Holy Spirit is the one who came upon Joshua in (Num. 27:18).
33. The Holy Spirit is the one who came upon Othniel in (Judges 3:10).
34. The Holy Spirit is the one who came upon Gideon in (Judges 6:34).
35. The Holy Spirit is the one who came upon Jephthah in (Judges 11:29).
36. The Holy Spirit is the one who came upon Samson in (Judges 14:6, 19).
37. The Holy Spirit is the one who came upon Saul in (1 Sam. 10:10).
38. The Holy Spirit is the one who came upon David in (1 Sam. 16:13).
39. The Holy Spirit is the one who came upon Elijah in (1 Kings 18:12).
40. The Holy Spirit is the one who came upon Elisha in (2 Kings 2:15).
41. The Holy Spirit is the one who came upon Zechariah the high priest in (2 Chron. 24:20).
42. The Holy Spirit is the one who came upon Israel's elders in (Number 11:25).

43. The Holy Spirit is the one who led Israel through the wilderness (Neh. 9:20).
44. The Holy Spirit is the one who will minister to Israel during the millennial reign (Zech. 12:10; Ezek. 37:13-14).
45. The Holy Spirit is the one who restrains the power of satan (2 Thessa. 2:7-14).
46. The Holy Spirit is the one who provided the Saviour with His earthly body (Luke 1:35; Matt. 1:18-20).
47. The Holy Spirit is the anointed Saviour (Matt. 3:16; Luke 4:18; Acts 10:38; Heb. 1:9).
48. The Holy Spirit is the one who directed the Saviour to be tempted by satan (Mat. 4:1).
49. The Holy Spirit is the one who empowered the Saviour (Matt. 12:28).
50. The Holy Spirit is the one who caused the Saviour to sorrow (John 11:33).
51. The Holy Spirit is the one who caused the Saviour to rejoice (Luke 10:21).
52. The Holy Spirit is the one who led the Saviour to Calvary (Heb. 9:14).
53. The Holy Spirit is the one who raised the body of the Saviour (Rom. 8:11).
54. The Holy Spirit is the one who convicts the unsaved person of sin, righteousness and judgement (Acts 2:1-4).
55. The Holy Spirit is the one who gave birth to the church (Acts 2:1-4).

56. The Holy Spirit is the who inspires the worship service of the church (Phil 3:3).
57. The Holy Spirit is the one who directs the church missionary works (Acts 8:29).
58. The Holy Spirit is the one who aids the church singing service (Eph. 5:18-19).
59. The Holy Spirit is the one who appoints the church preachers (Acts 20:28).
60. The Holy Spirit is the one who anoints the church preachers (1 Cor. 2:4).
61. The Holy Spirit is the one who warns church members (1 Tim. 4:1).
62. The Holy Spirit is the one who determines the church decisions (Acts 15:28).
63. The Holy Spirit is the one who directs the church evangelistic attempts (Rev. 22:17).
64. The Holy Spirit is the one who is able to condone or condemn the church (Rev. 2:7).
65. The Holy Spirit is the one who regenerates the believing sinner (Tit. 3:5).
66. The Holy Spirit is the one who baptises the believers (Rom. 6:3-4).
67. The Holy Spirit is the one who indwells the believers (John 14:16).
68. The Holy Spirit is the one who seals the believers (2 Cor. 1:22).
69. The Holy Spirit is the one who fills the believer (Acts 2:4).

70. The Holy Spirit is the one who conforms believers to the image of Christ (2 Cor. 3:18).
71. The Holy Spirit is the one who strengthens the believers' new nature (Eph. 3:16).
72. The Holy Spirit is the one who reveals biblical truths to believers (1 Cor. 2:10).
73. The Holy Spirit is the one who assures believers concerning salvation and service (Rom. 8:16).
74. The Holy Spirit is the one who gives believers liberty (Rom. 8:2).
75. The Holy Spirit is the one who fills the mouth of believers with appropriate things (Mark 3:11).
76. The Holy Spirit is the one who prays for believers (Rom. 8:26).
77. The Holy Spirit is the one who guides believers (John 16:13).
78. The Holy Spirit is the one who teaches believers (1 John 2:27).
79. The Holy Spirit is the one who empowers believers for witnessing (Acts 1:8).
80. The Holy Spirit is the one who imparts the love of Christ to believers, and through the believers (Rom. 5:5).
81. The Holy Spirit is the one who will someday raise the bodies of all departed believers (Rom. 8:11).

SPIRITUAL POWER?

WHAT IS SPIRITUAL POWER?

<u>MEMORY VERSE</u>

Psalm 62:11: "God hath spoken once; twice have I heard this; that power belongeth unto God."

TEXT Acts 1

INTRODUCTION It is becoming increasingly clear, that 'ice-cream' Christianity, laziness, slumbering prayers and low-spiritual energy will not get us anywhere. It is tragic to note that our current generation is a powerless one. In many situations, the judge has become the accused, and the servants have taken over the horses of the masters.

One of the greatest needs of today's church is bringing down the power of God. We need to demonstrate to this dying unbelieving world, that there can still be signs and wonders which convince people that, with God, nothing is impossible. We need to show to the world the manifestation of the kingdom of God to destroy the works of the devil. We need to turn the world upside down, by displaying the raw power of God. We need to display the supernatural power to solve human problems. We need to heal the sick, cleanse the lepers, raise the dead, cast out demons and bring salvation and deliverance to souls in satanic bondage.

More than at any other time, we need to bring down the fire power of God against the enemy. Why do we need to bring down the power of God? Demonic activities are in a terrible rage. Sins, sicknesses, diseases, curses, and untold problems are mounting and increasing daily. There are a lot of sufferings, poverty and lack in the world. Occult and satanic powers are nakedly displaying their powers. We therefore cannot afford to be powerless in the face of these assaults. It is an insult on your salvation for Pentecostal witchcraft, hypnotism, magic, voodoo, charms and fetish powers, to prosper in the life of a child of God.

Although there is restlessness and pressure mounted upon many for moving forward, many find it impossible to enter into the school of power. While evil men are waxing stronger and stronger, our powerlessness is becoming legendary.

WHAT IS POWER?

Power is an interesting word to define. The difficulty in defining power leads man to classify the different powers as ways of defining it. Powers are therefore classified into: solar power, physical power, technological power, spiritual power, material power, economic power, cultural power, political power, military power. Some even talk of bottom power, money power, magical power, mystical power, etc. There are also such satanic powers as fetish power, juju power, ogbanje power, babalawo power, etc. When men define power, they are talking about:

1. Ability to do or act.
2. Capability of doing or accomplishing something.
3. Political or economic strength.
4. The person or thing that possesses or exercises authority or influence.
5. A military force.
6. Vital energy to make choices and decisions.
7. Capacity to overcome.
8. A specific capacity.
9. Other capacities: to speak, convince, argue, charm, mesmerise, cause trouble, etc.
10. Power is the faculty or capacity to act effectively.
11. Forcefulness.
12. Ability to exercise control.
13. Strength or force exerted or capable of being exerted.
14. Applied force.
15. Intensity.
16. Mechanical energy.
17. Might.
18. Muscle.
19. Omnipotence.
20. Potency.
21. Potential.
22. Competence.
23. Dynamism.
24. Effectiveness.

25. Efficacy.
26. Endowment.
27. Faculty.
28. Function.
29. Influence.
30. Potentiality.
31. Qualification.
32. Skill.
33. Talent.
34. Virtue

WHAT IS SPIRITUAL POWER?

Power is like beauty. If you have to tell people that you are beautiful, then you are not. The only language the enemy respects is the language of power. The Bible is the only book that describes power accurately. The Bible makes us to understand that God is the ultimate source of power (Heb 4:12; Rom. 1:16; 1 Cor. 1:18; James 5:16-18; Rev. 12:11; Acts 1:8; Philp 3:10) and identifies power with the following characteristics:

1. The fullness of Christ dwelling in you (Col. 2:9).
2. Ability to go extra mile (Matt. 5:41).
3. Ability to turn the left cheek (Luke 6:29).
4. Ability to love those who do not love you (Matt. 5:44).
5. Ability to act and not react, when you are offended .
6. Being endued you with the capability to die and for Christ to reign in you (Gal. 2:20).

7. Being worthy, for the Lord to depend on you anywhere you are (Job 1:8).
8. The ability to remain unpolluted by the present world (Heb. 12:1).
9. Having access to the secrets or mysteries of God and remove obstacles in your way (Amos 3:7).
10. Ability to keep your flesh under control (1 Cor. 9:27).
11. Ability to be silent in the face of provocation (Isa. 53:7).
12. Being filled with the Holy Spirit (Acts 1:8).
13. Power to put your enemy to flight (Deut. 28:7).
14. Ability to remove obstacles in your way(Matt. 17:20).
15. Ability to move in supernatural gifts (1 Cor. 12).
16. Being truly broken (John 12:24).

DIFFERENCES BETWEEN POWER AND AUTHORITY :

1. Authority comes from the Word of God, that is, what God has said (Psalm 138:2).
2. Power comes from the anointing of the Holy Spirit (Acts 1:8).
3. Authority is exercised in the name of Jesus (Phil 2:9-10).
4. Power is operated by the anointing (Isa. 10:27; Acts 10:38).
5. Authority is given to every Christian without measure (Mark 16:17).

6. Power is given, according to self-crucifixion and faith (Gal. 2:20; 1 Cor. 15:31).
7. Authority is received by being born again (John 3:3).
8. Power is by living and moving in the realm of the spirit (1 Cor. 12).
9. Authority expresses your legal right as a Christian (Rom 6).
10. Power enforces your legal right as a Christian (Acts 16).
11. Authority is useless without power to punish.
12. Authority without power is a disaster.

6:00AM

PRAYER WATCH 1

6:00AM

Confessions:

Jer. 32:27

Aggresive Praise and Worship

Prayer Points:

1. Father, I thank You for Your resurrection power.
2. I thank You for Your power that is able to create and re-create.
3. Lord, send Your fire to the foundations of my life, in the name of Jesus.
4. Every evil marriage covenant in my life, break by the power in the blood of Jesus.
5. Let the blood of Jesus flush out every dark initiation and covenant in my life, in the name of Jesus.

6. Holy Ghost fire, destroy every evil consumption and contamination through food and sex physically and spiritually, in the name of Jesus.
7. I release my reproductive organs from any witchcraft cage, in the name of Jesus.
8. I release my reproductive organs from any evil padlock, in the name of Jesus.
9. I release my reproductive organs from any evil chain, in the name of Jesus.
10. I reject every curse of unfruitfulness in marriage, in the name of Jesus.
11. I reverse every curse of unfruitfulness in marriage, in the name of Jesus.
12. I revoke every curse of unfruitfulness in marriage, in the name of Jesus.
13. Let every tree planted over my umbilical cord and foreskin catch fire, in the name of Jesus.
14. Any power contesting against my children, die, in the name of Jesus.
15. I command my children to come to me by fire, in the name of Jesus.

16. Every dead organ in my body receive resurrection power, in the name of Jesus.
17. Every dead organ in my body, receive life now, in the name of Jesus.
18. Thou power of impotence and low sperm count in my life, break, in the name of Jesus.
19. Spirits of impotence and low sperm count, loose your hold upon my life, in the name of Jesus.
20. Every satanic manipulation of my life and body system, die, in the name of Jesus.
21. Every high sugar content in my body, be neutralised by the blood of Jesus.
22. Let my nervous and muscular system receive strength, in the name of Jesus.
23. Every evil programme against my reproduction, catch fire, in the name of Jesus.
24. Any problem in my life, that is resisting solution, catch fire, in the name of Jesus.
25. O Lord, let my shame be turned into glory, in the name of Jesus.
26. I fire back every arrow of deafness, in the name of Jesus.

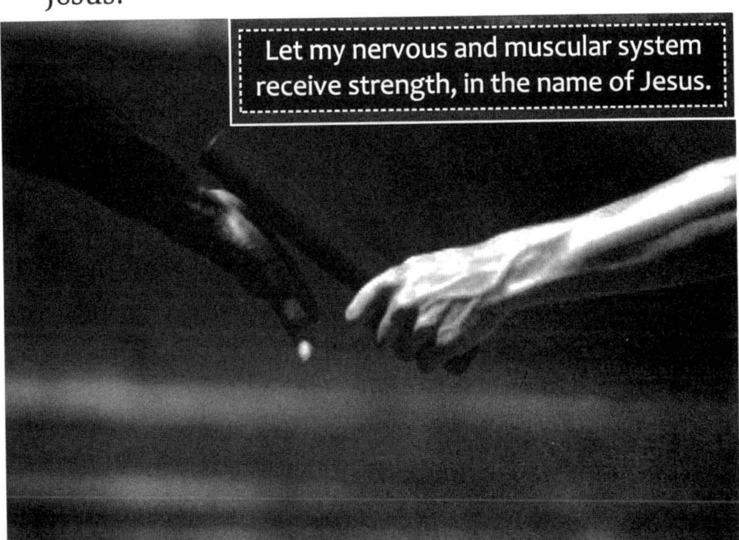

27. I recover my reproductive organs from any marine and occult altar, in the name of Jesus.
28. Holy Ghost fire, strengthen me to recover my possessions, in the name of Jesus.
29. O God, arise and speak the words of power into every organ of my body, in the name of Jesus.
30. I cancel every evil clinical prophesy against my life, in the name of Jesus.
31. Every blood covenant speaking against my reproductive organs, break, in the name of Jesus.
32. I sprinkle the blood of Jesus upon my body - from the top of my head to the soles of my feet.
33. I paralyse all satanic oppressors delegated against me with the blood of Jesus
34. I curse every work of darkness in my life to dry to the roots by the blood of Jesus
35. I defeat, paralyse and erase every sickness demon by the blood of Jesus.
36. I overcome every spirit of infirmity by the blood of the Lamb.
37. No spirit, power or personality shall be able to put any sickness on me because I am redeemed by the blood of the Lamb.
38. Let the blood of Jesus speak peace unto every organ in my body
39. Every root of infirmities in my life, dry up, in the name of Jesus.
40. Every citadel of sickness in my life, catch fire, in the name of Jesus.
41. I reject every evil clinical prophecy, in the name of Jesus.

42. Every power speaking death and malfunctioning into any organ of my body, die, in the name of Jesus.
43. O God, arise with Your healing power and visit me, in the name of Jesus.
44. Any curse or covenant, that is aiding sickness in my life, be broken by the power in the blood of Jesus.
45. I drink the blood of Jesus and I command the roots of sicknesses in my life to dry up, in the name of Jesus.
46. Let my body be redeemed from the power of sickness and diseases, in the name of Jesus.
47. Any evil association against my health, scatter, in the name of Jesus.
48. Every witchcraft caldron cooking my health, catch fire, in the name of Jesus.
49. Every witchcraft ordinance written against my health, die, in the name of Jesus.
50. Thank God for your healing.

9:00AM

PRAYER WATCH 2

9:00AM

Confessions:

Isa. 53:5

Aggressive Praise and Worship

Prayer Points:

1. Thank You Father for the benefits and provision of the blood of Jesus.
2. I apply the blood of Jesus to every hidden sickness in my life.
3. I sprinkle the blood of Jesus upon my body - from the top of my head to the soles of my feet.
4. I paralyse all satanic oppressors delegated against me with the blood of Jesus.
5. I hold the blood of Jesus as a shield against any power of sickness in my life, in Jesus' name.

6. Let every door that I have opened to the enemy be closed forever with the blood of Jesus.
7. Through the blood of Jesus, I have been redeemed out of every sickness.
8. Through the blood of Jesus I am healed.
9. Through the blood of Jesus, I have the life of God in me.
10. I paralyse and cut off the head of my Goliath with the blood of Jesus.
11. Anything in me that is not of God, I do not want you. Depart, in the name of Jesus.
12. Let the blood of Jesus, stand between me and any sickness.
13. I curse every work of darkness in my life to dry to the roots by the blood of Jesus.
14. I defeat, paralyse and erase . . . (pick from the under listed) by the blood of Jesus.
    - spirit of infirmity
    - untimely death
    - inherited sicknesses
    - dream attackers
15. Let the power of the blood of Jesus be released on my behalf and let it speak against every dead bone in my life.

16. Let the power of the blood of Jesus be released on my behalf and let it speak against every stubborn mountain in my life.
17. I draw a circle of the blood of Jesus around me against every arrow of infirmity.
18. I overcome every spirit of infirmity by the blood of the Lamb.
19. No spirit, power or personality shall be able to put any sickness on me because I am redeemed by the blood of the Lamb.
20. Let the blood of Jesus speak confusion into the camp of the enemy.
21. Let the blood of Jesus speak destruction unto every evil growth in my life.
22. Let the blood of Jesus speak disappearance unto every infirmity in my life.
23. Let the blood of Jesus speak peace unto every organ in my body.
24. Let the blood of Jesus speak healing unto every organ of my body.
25. Let the blood of Jesus dry up every evil tree used against me.
26. I render every evil power militating against my health impotent by the blood of Jesus.
27. Let the blood of Jesus minister defeat to every evil work in my life.
28. Let the blood of Jesus bring down to nothing any evil work in my life.
29. I minister death unto the enemy of good health in my life by the blood of Jesus.
30. I bind the staying power of any problem by the blood of Jesus.
31. I hold the blood of Jesus against any evil spirit working against me.

32. I hold the blood of Jesus against you, spirit of. (mention the sickness in your life). You have to flee.
33. I hold the blood of Jesus against the spirit of stagnation in any area of my life.
34. I hold the blood of Jesus against demonic delay of my miracles.
35. I hold the blood of Jesus against failure at the edge of success.
36. I hold the blood of Jesus against lack of good helpers.
37. I hold the blood of Jesus against fruitless efforts in my life.
38. I hold the blood of Jesus against occupying wrong positions.
39. I hold the blood of Jesus against every delayed and denied promotion.
40. I hold the blood of Jesus against dead accounts.
41. I hold the blood of Jesus against evil diversion.
42. I hold the blood of Jesus against lost foreign benefits.
43. I hold the blood of Jesus against satanic prophecies.
44. I hold the blood of Jesus against vagabond anointing.
45. I hold the blood of Jesus against profit starvation.

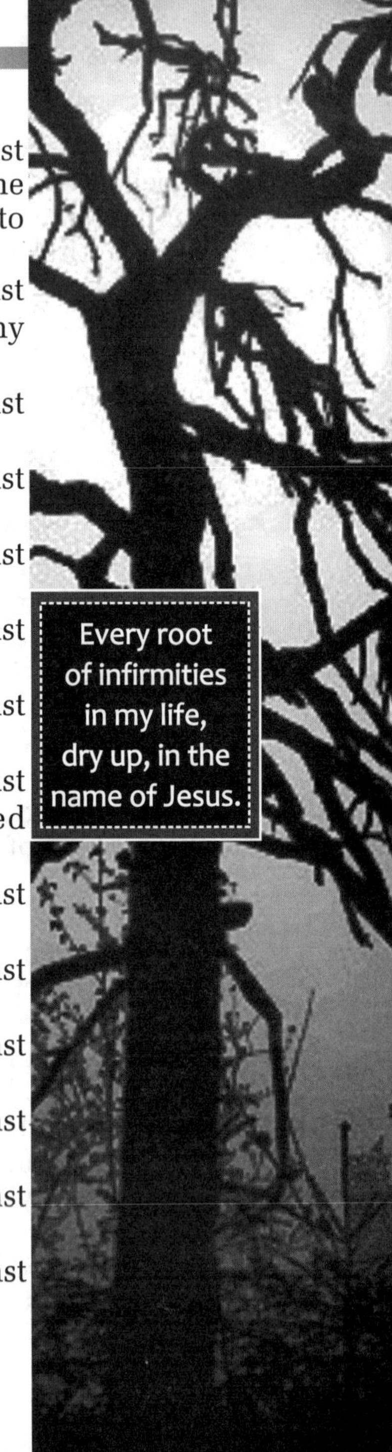

46. I hold the blood of Jesus against tortoise and snail anointing.
47. I am healed by the stripes of Jesus.
48. Any sin in my life that is bringing sickness to me, die, in the name of Jesus.
49. Holy Ghost fire, purge the foundation of my life, in the name of Jesus.
50. Let the power of revival fall upon my body, in the name of Jesus.
51. By faith, I touch the hem of the garment of Jesus, and I receive my healing now, in the name of Jesus.
52. Every evil food causing sickness in my body, die, in the name of Jesus.
53. Every curse afflicting me with sickness, be broken by the blood of Jesus.
54. Every root of infirmities in my life, dry up, in the name of Jesus.
55. Let the power of resurrection come upon my life now, in the name of Jesus.
56. Every demonic connection monitoring sickness in my life, break, in the name of Jesus.
57. Oh Lord, heal me and I shall be healed, in the name of Jesus.
58. Every power assigned to waste my life, be wasted, in the name of Jesus.
59. Let signs and wonders appear in my life, in the name of Jesus.
60. Every physical and spiritual hindrance to my healing, be removed by fire, in the name of Jesus.
61. Every evil mark delaying my healing, die, in the name of Jesus.

62. Holy Ghost fire, visit me with your signs and wonders, in the name of Jesus.
63. Every citadel of sickness in my life, catch fire, in the name of Jesus.
64. Every agent of sickness in my body, die, in the name of Jesus.
65. I receive divine immunity against all sorts of sicknesses, in the name of Jesus.

Prayer
WATCH
3

12:00PM

PRAYER WATCH 3

12:00 NOON

Confessions:

Exodus 15:26; Psalm 91:1-16

Praise Worship

Prayer Points:

1. Every organ of my body, cooperate with the blood of Jesus.
2. Revival power, resurrection power, rejuvenating power, come upon every organ of my body, in the name of Jesus.
3. Any organ of my body that has lost its function, resume your functions now, in the name of Jesus.
4. Blood of Jesus, speak life into my head, my heart, my liver, my kidney, my bladder, my womb, etc, in the name of Jesus.
5. I reject every evil clinical prophecy, in the name of Jesus.

6. I pull down every satanic bewitchment upon any organ of my body, in the name of Jesus.
7. Every pronouncement of man about my health that is contrary to my life, I cancel it by the blood of Jesus.
8. By the word of God, through which all things were created, let my life experience divine power, in the name of Jesus.
9. Holy Ghost fire, renew my strength, in the name of Jesus.
10. Blood of Jesus, renew my strength, in the name of Jesus.
11. My Father, make me a mysterious wonder, in the name of Jesus.
12. Where is the Lord God of Elijah, arise and reorganize my organ for uncommon testimonies, in the name of Jesus.

13. Every power speaking death and malfunctioning into any organ of my body, die, in the name of Jesus.
14. I receive fresh energy, fresh fire, fresh power into every organ of my body, in the name of Jesus.
15. Father, dispatch Your heavenly surgeons to work upon my life, and make impossible possible, in the name of Jesus.
16. By the power of the God of Elijah, let uncommon breakthroughs manifest in my life, in the name of Jesus.
17. Let the Prince of Peace speak peace unto every storm in my life, in the name of Jesus.
18. O God arise with Your healing power and visit me, in the name of Jesus.
19. Every altar of affliction of sickness, catch fire, in the name of Jesus.
20. Any curse or covenant, that is aiding sickness in my life, be broken by the power in the blood of Jesus.
21. Any sickness on my body, be shaken off by fire, in the name of Jesus.
22. Every mountain of sickness, be rolled away by fire, in the name of Jesus.
23. I drink the blood of Jesus and I command the roots of sicknesses in my life to dry up, in the name of Jesus.
24. Every plantation of sickness in my body, catch fire, in the name of Jesus.
25. Every agent of sickness in my body, come out and die, in the name of Jesus.
26. Let my body be redeemed from the power of sickness and diseases, in the name of Jesus.

27. Let the power of death and hell behind any sickness in my body, loose your hold and die, in the name of Jesus.
28. I shall not die but live to declare the works of God, in the name of Jesus.
29. Every water of affliction of sickness flowing into my life, be cut off, in the name of Jesus.
30. Any evil association against my health, scatter, in the name of Jesus.
31. Any evil weapon fashioned against my health, die, in the name of Jesus.
32. Every fire of sickness tormenting my life, East wind, blow them away, in the name of Jesus.
33. Let the fire of Holy Ghost melt away sicknesses in my body, in the name of Jesus.
34. Every power of sickness and diseases on my body, die by fire, in the name of Jesus.
35. Every witchcraft cauldron cooking my health, catch fire, in the name of Jesus.
36. Let my light break forth and my health spring forth speedily, in the name of Jesus.
37. I bear in my body the mark of the blood of Jesus, let sickness flee away from my habitation, in the name of Jesus.
38. Every witchcraft ordinance written against my health, die, in the name of Jesus.
39. Every spirit eating me from inside, die, in the name of Jesus.
40. Jesus, the great Physician, make Yourself known to me as I enter the hospital.
41. O Lord, come into this house with Your hands and touch the sick

42. O Lord, restore health and wholeness by fire.
43. O Lord, heal every hidden evil memory.
44. Any power damaging my health, die, in the name of Jesus.
45. I deliver myself from evil influences of diseases, in the name of Jesus.
46. Let Your Spirit, O Lord, minister healing to my life.
47. Let the healing anointing be upon my home, in the name of Jesus.
48. Every barrier to the movement of healing gifts to operate on my behalf, be broken, in the name of Jesus.
49. I sanctify every equipment and drug that would be used for me and on me, in the name of Jesus.
50. Every eater of flesh and drinker of blood in the hospital, my body is not your candidate, in the name of Jesus
51. I cover the whole of the hospital with the blood of Jesus.

52. O Lord, build the hedge of the blood of Jesus around my life.
53. I shall not die but live to declare the works of God, in the name of Jesus.
54. Let divine wisdom enter into those who will minister to me for medical and nursing care, in the name of Jesus.
55. By the power that divided the Red Sea, let my weaknesses be banished and let my health be restored, in the name of Jesus.
56. I will live to glorify Your holy name, in the name of Jesus.
57. I cover all the members of staff with the blood of Jesus.
58. Wonderful Father, I put myself into Your hands before the operation, in the name of Jesus.
59. Thank God for your healing.

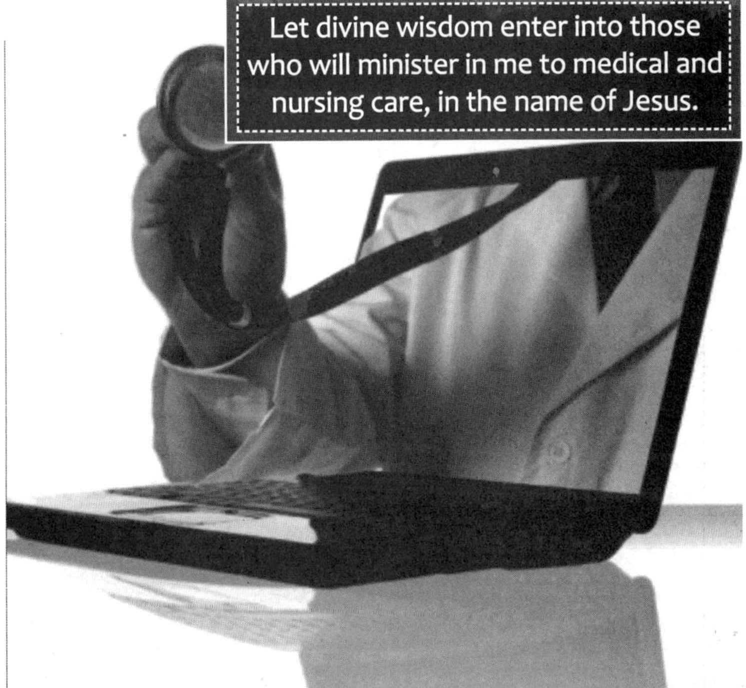

3:00PM

PRAYER WATCH 4

3:00PM

Confessions:

Psalm 27:1-2: *The Lord is my light and my salvation; whom shall I fear? the Lord is the strength of my life; of whom shall I be afraid? [2] When the wicked, even mine enemies and my foes, came upon me to eat up my flesh, they stumbled and fell.*

Isaiah 49:24-26: *Shall the prey be taken from the mighty, or the lawful captive delivered? [25] But thus saith the Lord, Even the captives of the mighty shall be taken away, and the prey of the terrible shall be delivered: for I will contend with him that contendeth with thee, and I will save thy children. [26] And I will feed them that oppress thee with their own flesh; and* *they shall be drunken with their own blood, as with sweet wine: and all flesh shall know that I the Lord am thy Saviour and thy Redeemer, the mighty One of Jacob.*

Isaiah 53:4-5: *Surely he hath borne our griefs, and carried our sorrows: yet we did esteem him stricken, smitten of God, and afflicted. [5] But he was wounded for our transgressions, he was bruised for our iniquities: the chastisement of our peace was upon him; and with his stripes we are healed.*

Deut. 7:15: *And the Lord will take away from thee all sickness, and will put none of the evil diseases of Egypt, which thou knowest, upon thee; but will lay them upon all them that hate thee.*

Aggressive Praise and Worship

Prayer Points:

1. I arrest any serpent of infirmity troubling my body, in the name of Jesus.
2. Destructive infirmities, hear the word of the Lord. Die, in the name of Jesus.
3. I cut off the tentacles of internal disease spreading in my body, in the name of Jesus.
4. Power base of infirmity, dry up and die, in the name of Jesus.

5. Health arresters, be arrested by fire, in the name of Jesus.
6. Holy Ghost fire, melt away every infirmity in my body organs, in the name of Jesus.
7. I fire back, every arrow of affliction tormenting my body, in the name of Jesus.
8. I kill every killer disease by the power in the blood of Jesus.
9. The battle of the terrible and the mighty against my health, expire, in the name of Jesus.
10. Thou Great Physician, Jesus Christ, heal me now, in the name of Jesus.
11. Yokes of infirmity, break to pieces, in the name of Jesus.
12. Authority of infirmity scorpions over my life, terminate, in the name of Jesus.
13. Every cell in my body, hear the word of the Lord. Reject evil commands, in the name of Jesus.
14. Let my bodily organs become too hot for any disease to handle, in the name of Jesus.
15. I charge my body with the fire of the Holy Ghost, in the name of Jesus.
16. Blood of Jesus, sanitise my body and make me whole, in the name of Jesus.
17. Eaters of flesh assigned against me, fall down and die, in the name of Jesus.
18. My flesh, my blood, reject the voice of death, in the name of Jesus.
19. Any power feeding on my flesh, come out and die, in the name of Jesus.

20. Agents of killer infirmities, I kill you now, in the name of Jesus.
21. My blood, hear the word of the Lord. Reject visible and invisible agents of infirmity, in the name of Jesus.
22. Any power assigned to eat me up, die, in the name of Jesus.
23. Every demon termite eating my body, die by fire, in the name of Jesus.
24. Every witchcraft poison in my body, dry up and die, in the name of Jesus.
25. Every curse of consumption afflicting my life, break, in the name of Jesus.
26. Every clearing pestilence, scatter, in the name of Jesus.
27. Blood of Jesus, pump out any stranger in my body, in the name of Jesus.
28. My body organs, reject the voice of early death, in the name of Jesus.
29. Strangers from the grave, clear out of my body, in the name of Jesus.
30. My life, reject the strangers that smite unto death, in the name of Jesus.

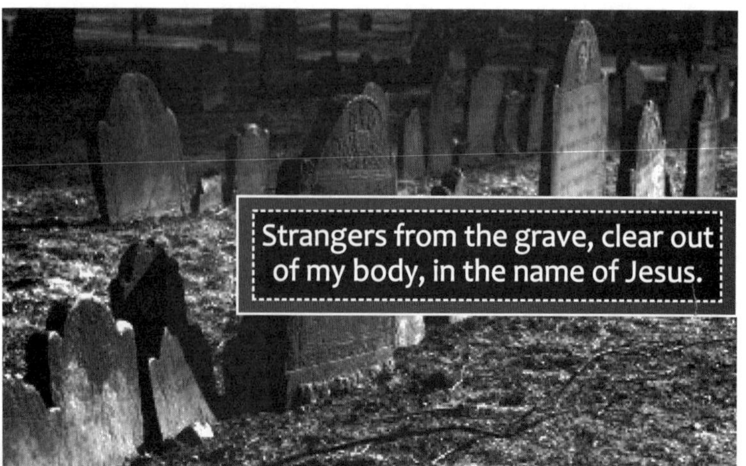

31. I break the yoke of the invisible destroyers, in the name of Jesus.
32. Every venom of the serpent and scorpion eating up my flesh, dry up now, in the name of Jesus.
33. I drink the blood of Jesus. (Say this 21 times.)
34. Let God arise and let my infirmity be scattered, in the name of Jesus.
35. I bind and cast out every agent of weakness, in the name of Jesus.
36. Parasites, viruses and bacteria of infirmity, my body is not your candidate. Die, in the name of Jesus.
37. Bewitchment of my flesh, blood and bones, terminate, in the name of Jesus.
38. Wasting powers, depart from my life, in the name of Jesus.
39. O God, arise and make me whole, in the name of Jesus.
40. My Father, arise in Your power and have mercy on me, in the name of Jesus.

6:00 PM

PRAYER WATCH 5

6:00PM

Confession:

Psalm 103:3: *Who forgiveth all thine iniquities; who healeth all thy diseases;*

Psalm 107:20: *He sent his word, and healed them, and delivered them from their destructions.*

Psalm 138:1-8: *I will praise thee with my whole heart: before the gods will I sing praise unto thee. I will worship toward thy holy temple, and praise thy name for thy lovingkindness and for thy truth: for thou hast magnified thy word above all thy name. In the day when I cried thou answeredst me, and strengthenedst me with strength in my soul. All the kings of the earth shall praise thee, O Lord, when they hear the words of thy mouth. Yea, they shall sing in the ways of the Lord: for great is the glory of the Lord. Though the Lord be high, yet hath he respect unto the lowly: but the proud he knoweth afar off. Though I walk in the midst of trouble, thou wilt* *revive me: thou shalt stretch forth thine hand against the wrath of mine enemies, and thy right hand shall save me. The Lord will perfect that which concerneth me: thy mercy, O Lord, endureth for ever: forsake not the works of thine own hands.*

Proverbs 12:18: *There is that speaketh like the piercings of a sword: but the tongue of the wise is health.*

Jeremiah 17:14: *Heal me, Lord, and I shall be healed; save me, and I shall be saved: for thou art my praise.*

Jeremiah 33:6: *Behold, I will bring it health and cure, and I will cure them, and will reveal unto them the abundance of peace and truth.*

1Peter 3:12: *For the eyes of the Lord are over the righteous, and his ears are open unto their prayers: but the face of the Lord is against them that do evil.*

James 5:16: *Confess your faults one to another, and pray one for another, that ye may be healed. The effectual fervent prayer of a righteous man availeth much.*

3John 2: *Beloved, I wish above all things that thou mayest prosper and be in health, even as thy soul prospereth.*

Praise Worship:

Prayer Points:

1. Every power planning to kill, steal and destroy my body, release me by fire, in the name of Jesus.
2. Every spirit of tiredness, release me. In the name of Jesus.

3. Every spirit of hypertension, come out with all your roots, in the name of Jesus.
4. Every bondage of diabetic spirits, come out with all your roots, in the name of Jesus.
5. Any evil power running through my body, loose your hold, in the name of Jesus.
6. Every evil power touching my brain, release me, in Jesus' name.
7. Every tentacle spirit moving about in my body, come out by fire, in the name of Jesus.
8. Every spirit of migraine and headache, come out by fire, in the name of Jesus.
9. Every dark spirit working against the kingdom of God in my life, come out by fire, in the name of Jesus.
10. Every power working on my eyes and reducing my vision, be eliminated completely, in the name of Jesus.
11. Every demon of insulin deficiency, depart by fire, in Jesus' name.
12. Every spirit of hypertension, release my liver, in the name of Jesus.
13. Every evil power planning to amputate my leg, I bury you alive, in the name of Jesus.
14. Every spirit of hypertension, release my bladder, in Jesus' name.
15. Every spirit of excessive urination, release me, in Jesus' name.
16. Every spirit of hypertension, release my skin and ears, in the name of Jesus.
17. Every spirit of itching, depart, in the name of Jesus.
18. Every spirit of hypertension, release my lungs, in the name of Jesus.

19. Every spirit of hypertension, release my reproductive areas, in the name of Jesus.
20. I release myself from every spirit of drowsiness, tiredness and impaired vision, I bind you and cast you out, in Jesus' name.
21. Every spirit of infirmity generating tiredness, loose your hold, in the name of Jesus.
22. Every spirit of excessive thirst and hunger, I bind you and cast you out, in the name of Jesus.
23. I bind every spirit of loss of weight, in the name of Jesus.
24. I bind every spirit of rashes, in the name of Jesus.
25. I bind every spirit of slow healing of cuts and bruises, in the name of Jesus.
26. I bind every spirit of bed-wetting, in the name of Jesus.
27. I bind every spirit of enlargement of the liver, in Jesus' name.
28. I bind every spirit of kidney disease, in the name of Jesus.
29. I bind every spirit of gangrene, in the name of Jesus.
30. I bind every spirit of hardening of the arteries, in Jesus' name.

31. I bind every spirit of confusion, in the name of Jesus.
32. I bind every spirit of convulsion, in the name of Jesus.
33. I bind every spirit of loss of consciousness, in the name of Jesus.
34. The spirit of the fear of death, depart from my life, in the name of Jesus.
35. The evil doorkeeper of insulin, loose your hold, in the name of Jesus.
36. Every power destroying insulin in my body, I bind you and cast you out, in the name of Jesus.
37. Every power hindering the co-ordination between my brain and my mouth, I bind you and cast you out, in the name of Jesus.
38. Every spirit of torment, release me, in the name of Jesus.
39. Every power attacking my blood sugar, loose your hold, in the name of Jesus.
40. I break every curse of eating and drinking blood from ten generations backward on both sides of my family lines, in the name of Jesus.
41. Every door opened to diabetic spirits, be closed by the blood of Jesus.
42. Every inherited blood disease, loose your hold, in Jesus' name.
43. All bloodline curses, be broken, in the name of Jesus.
44. Every curse of breaking the skin of my body unrighteously, be broken, in the name of Jesus.
45. I bind every demon in my pancreas and I cast them out, in the name of Jesus.
46. Any power affecting my vision, I bind you, in the name of Jesus.
47. Every satanic arrow in my blood vessel, come out by fire, in the name of Jesus.

48. Every demon of stroke, come out with all your roots, in the name of Jesus.
49. Every spirit of confusion, loose your hold, in the name of Jesus.
50. Anything inhibiting my ability to read and meditate on the word of God, be uprooted, in the name of Jesus.
51. I bind and cast out every spirit of (convulsion - guilt - abdominal problems - fear - hopelessness -palsy - impotence - animal - candour - swelling - stress - worry - anxiety - deafness - high blood pressure - nerve destruction - kidney destruction), in Jesus' name.
52. I bind and cast out familiar spirits moving through family bloodlines to cause hypertension and other sicknesses, in Jesus' name.
53. I command every evil plantation in my life: come out with all your roots in the name of Jesus! (Lay your hands on your stomach and keep repeating the emphasised area.)
54. I cough out and vomit any food eaten from the table of the devil, in the name of Jesus. (Cough them out and vomit them in faith. Prime the expulsion.)
55. Let all negative materials circulating in my blood stream, be evacuated, in the name of Jesus.
56. I drink the blood of Jesus. (Physically swallow and drink it in faith. Do so for some time.)
57. (Lay one hand on your head and the other on your stomach or navel and begin to pray like this) Holy Ghost fire, burn from the top of my head to the sole of my feet. (Begin to mention every organ of your body; your kidney, liver, intestines, blood, etc. You must not rush at this level, because the fire will actually come and you may start feeling the heat).
58. Let the blood of Jesus be transfused into my blood vessels, in the name of Jesus.

59. I command every agent of disease in my blood and body organs to die, in the name of Jesus.
60. Let my blood reject every evil foreign entity, in the name of Jesus.
61. Holy Spirit, speak deliverance and healing into my life, in the name of Jesus.
62. Let the blood of Jesus speak disappearance unto every infirmity in my life.
63. I hold the blood of Jesus against you spirit of (mention what is troubling you) you have to flee.
64. O Lord, let Your healing hand be stretched out upon my life now.
65. O Lord, let Your miracle hand be stretched out upon my life now.
66. O Lord, let Your deliverance hand be stretched out upon my life now.
67. I disannul every engagement with the spirit of death, in Jesus' name.
68. I rebuke every refuge of sickness, in the name of Jesus.
69. I destroy the grip and operation of sickness upon my life, in the name of Jesus.
70. Every knee of infirmity in my life, bow, in the name of Jesus.
71. O Lord, let my negativity be converted to positivity.
72. I command death upon any sickness in any area of my life, in the name of Jesus.
73. I shall see my sickness no more, in the name of Jesus.
74. Father Lord, let Your whirlwind scatter every vessel of infirmity fashioned against my life, in the name of Jesus.
75. Every spirit hindering my perfect healing, fall down and die now, in the name of Jesus.
76. Father Lord, let all death contractors begin to kill themselves, in the name of Jesus.

77. Father Lord, let every germ of infirmity in my body die, in the name of Jesus.
78. Father Lord, let every agent of sickness working against my health disappear, in the name of Jesus.
79. Every fountain of discomfort in my life, dry up now, in the name of Jesus.
80. Every dead organ in my body, receive life now, in the name of Jesus.
81. Father Lord, let my blood be transfused with the blood of Jesus to effect my perfect health, in the name of Jesus.
82. Every internal disorder, receive order, in the name of Jesus.

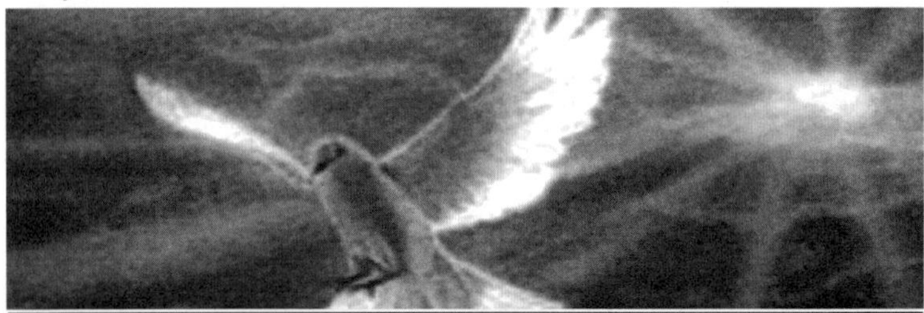

(Lay one hand on your head and the other on your stomach or navel and begin to pray like this) Holy Ghost fire, burn from the top of my head to the sole of my feet. (Begin to mention every organ of your body; your kidney, liver, intestines, blood, etc. You must not rush at this level, because the fire will actually come and you may start feeling the heat).

83. Every infirmity, come out with all your roots, in the name of Jesus.
84. I withdraw every conscious and unconscious cooperation with the devil, in the name of Jesus.
85. O Lord, let Your whirlwind blow away every wind of infirmity.

86. I release my body from every curse of infirmity, in the name of Jesus.
87. O Lord, let the blood of Jesus flush out every evil deposit from my blood.
88. I recover every organ of my body from every evil altar, in Jesus' name.
89. I withdraw my body from the manipulation of every caldron of darkness, in the name of Jesus.
90. Holy Ghost fire, destroy every stubborn agent of disease in my body, in the name of Jesus.
91. I arrest every demon of terminal disease, in the name of Jesus.
92. I cancel every clinical prophesy concerning my life, in the name of Jesus.
93. Holy Ghost fire, boil every infirmity out of my system, in the name of Jesus.
94. I cancel every witchcraft verdict against my life, in the name of Jesus.
95. O earth, vomit anything that has been buried inside you against my health, in the name of Jesus.
96. Every tree that infirmity has planted in my blood, be uprooted by fire, in the name of Jesus.
97. I command every witchcraft arrow to depart from my
    - spinal cord - spleen - navel - heart
    - throat - between the eyes - top of the head.
98. I bind every evil presence in my (reproductive, digestive, respiratory, nervous, skeletal, muscular, circulatory, endocrine, excretory) system, in the name of Jesus.
99. I break the backbone and destroy the root of every spirit speaking against me, in the name of Jesus.
100. Thank God for your healing.

9:00 PM

PRAYER WATCH 6

9:00 PM

Confession -

Rev. 12:11: *And they overcame him by the blood of the Lamb, and by the word of their testimony; and they loved not their lives unto the death.*

In the name of Jesus Christ, I am a beloved child of God. I believe in God, I believe in Jesus Christ and I believe in the blessed Holy Spirit Who is dwelling in the inside of me. I believe in the unshakeable and eternal power in the word of God. I believe that life and death are in my tongue. I believe that as I make this confession unto life with the power in my tongue, according to the words which the Lord has this day put in my mouth, I shall prosper. It is written that Jesus Christ offered His blood as a drink, and His flesh as bread that whosoever drinks and eats it shall not die forever. Now, with strong faith in my heart, I hold in my hand a cup containing the blood of the Lamb of

blood flush out of me all inherited or self-acquired evil deposits in my system. Let it purify my blood system. I eat with the heart of faith, the flesh of Jesus. For it is written, His flesh is bread indeed. I eat it now so that I can also eat with Him in His glory. As I eat and drink the flesh and blood of my Lord Jesus Christ, I renew my covenant with Him and I receive the life therein; for it is written, life is in the blood. Thus, I possess the life and the Spirit of Christ in me. Amen.

Praise Worship

Prayer Points:

1. Thank You Father for the benefits and provision of the blood of Jesus.
2. I apply the blood of Jesus to every hidden sickness in my life.
3. I sprinkle the blood of Jesus upon my body - from the top of my head to the soles of my feet.
4. I paralyse all satanic oppressors delegated against me with the blood of Jesus.
5. I hold the blood of Jesus as a shield against any power of sickness in my life, in Jesus' name.
6. Let every door that I have opened to the enemy be closed forever with the blood of Jesus.
7. Through the blood of Jesus, I have been redeemed out of every sickness.
8. Through the blood of Jesus I am healed.
9. Through the blood of Jesus, I have the life of God in me.

10. I paralyse and cut off the head of my Goliath with the blood of Jesus.
11. Anything in me that is not of God, I do not want you. Depart, in the name of Jesus.
12. Let the blood of Jesus, stand between me and any sickness.
13. I curse every work of darkness in my life to dry to the roots by the blood of Jesus.
14. I defeat, paralyse and erase . . . (pick from the under listed) by the blood of Jesus.
    - spirit of infirmity
    - untimely death
    - inherited sicknesses
    - dream attackers
15. Let the power of the blood of Jesus be released on my behalf and let it speak against every dead bone in my life.
16. Let the power of the blood of Jesus be released on my behalf and let it speak against every stubborn mountain in my life.
17. I draw a circle of the blood of Jesus around me against every arrow of infirmity.
18. I overcome every spirit of infirmity by the blood of the Lamb.

I sprinkle the blood of Jesus upon my body - from the top of my head to the soles of my feet.

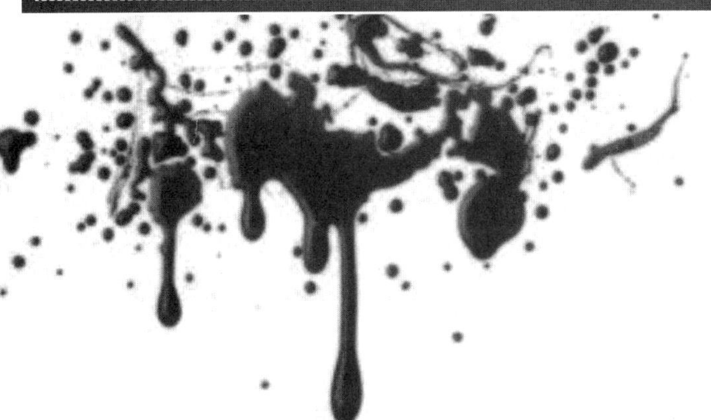

19. No spirit, power or personality shall be able to put any sickness on me because I am redeemed by the blood of the Lamb.
20. Let the blood of Jesus speak confusion into the camp of the enemy.
21. Let the blood of Jesus speak destruction unto every evil growth in my life.
22. Let the blood of Jesus speak disappearance unto every infirmity in my life.
23. Let the blood of Jesus speak peace unto every organ in my body.
24. Let the blood of Jesus speak healing unto every organ of my body.
25. Let the blood of Jesus dry up every evil tree used against me.
26. I render every evil power militating against my health impotent by the blood of Jesus.
27. Let the blood of Jesus minister defeat to every evil work in my life.
28. Let the blood of Jesus bring down to nothing any evil work in my life.
29. I minister death unto the enemy of good health in my life by the blood of Jesus.
30. I bind the staying power of any problem by the blood of Jesus.
31. I hold the blood of Jesus against any evil spirit working against me.
32. I hold the blood of Jesus against you spirit of . . . You have to flee. (Mention the sickness in your life)
33. I hold the blood of Jesus against the spirit of stagnation in any area of my life.

34. I hold the blood of Jesus against demonic delay of my miracles.
35. .I hold the blood of Jesus against failure at the edge of success.
36. I hold the blood of Jesus against lack of good helpers.
37. I hold the blood of Jesus against fruitless efforts in my life.
38. I hold the blood of Jesus against occupying wrong positions.
39. I hold the blood of Jesus against every delayed and denied promotion.
40. I hold the blood of Jesus against dead accounts.
41. I hold the blood of Jesus against evil diversion.
42. I hold the blood of Jesus against lost foreign benefits.
43. I hold the blood of Jesus against satanic prophecies.
44. I hold the blood of Jesus against vagabond anointing.
45. I hold the blood of Jesus against profit starvation.
46. I hold the blood of Jesus against tortoise and snail anointing.

Let the blood of Jesus minister defeat to every evil work in my life.

Prayer
WATCH
7

12:00AM

PRAYER WATCH 7

12:00AM

Confession -

Proverbs 4:20-22: *My son, attend to my words; incline thine ear unto my saying. 21Let them not depart from thine eyes; keep them in the midst of thine heart. 22For they are life unto those that find them, and health to all their flesh.*

2 Tim. 1:7: *For God hath not given us the spirit of fear; but of power, and of a sound mind.*

2 Tim. 3:3: *But the Lord is faithful, who shall stablish you, and keep you from evil.*

Matthew 15:13: *But he answered and said, Every plant, which my heavenly Father hath not planted, shall be rooted up.*

Mark 11:23: *For verily I say unto you, That whosoever shall say unto this mountain, Be thou removed, and be*

but shall believe that those things he saith shall come to pass; he shall have whatsoever he saith.

Mark 11:24: *Therefore I say unto you, What things soever ye desire, when ye pray, believe that ye receive them, and ye shall have them.*

Jeremiah 30:15-17: *Why criest thou for thine affliction? Thy sorrow is incurable for the multitude of thine iniquity: because thy sins were increased, I have done these thing unto thee. 16Therefore all they that devour thee shall be devoured; and all thine adversaries, every one of them, shall go into captivity; and they that spoil thee shall be a spoil, and all that prey upon thee will i give for a prey. 17For i will restore health unto thee, and i will heal thee of thy wounds, saith the LORD; because they called thee an Outcast, saying, This is Zion, whom no man seeketh after.*

Praise Worship

Prayer Points:

1. All the activities of silent killer in my body, die, in the name of Jesus.
2. You the symptom of cancer in any area of my body, die, in the name of Jesus.
3. Every evil growth in my body, i curse you to die, in the name of Jesus.
4. I fire back every arrow of cancer, in the name of Jesus.
5. Every abnormal production and uncontrollable behaviour of cells in my body, stop, in the name of Jesus.

6. I bind every spirit of death and hell, in the name of Jesus.
7. Every negative consequence of abnormal production of cells in my body, die, in the name of Jesus.
8. I shall not die but live to declare the works of God, in the name of Jesus.
9. You mass of extra tissue/tumour that has become malignant in my breast, be melted by the fire of God, in the name of Jesus.
10. Every demon of cancer, I bind you and cast you out, in the name of Jesus.
11. Every break away cancer cell from malignant tumour that has entered my bloodstream (Lymphatic system), be flushed away by the blood of Jesus.
12. Every vampire spirit, release my life, in the name of Jesus.
13. You the malignant tumour, go back to your own kind by fire, in the name of Jesus.
14. O Great Physician, deliver me now.
15. Every spread of cancer (metastasis) in my body, stop; and I command normalcy to my body system, in the name of Jesus.
16. Lay your hands on the affected part and pray like this:
    - Evil growth in my body, dry up and die, in the name of Jesus.
    - Satanic instructions to my body, be dismantled, in the name of Jesus.
    - Every poison in my body, come out through the mouth and the nose, in the name of Jesus.

- Every spirit behind this cancer, come out with all your roots, in the name of Jesus.
- Every cancer anchor in my body, be dismantled, in the name of Jesus.
- Every vehicle of cancer, crash, in the name of Jesus.
- Power of cancer, die, in the name of Jesus.
- Holy Ghost fire, burn away every cancer, in the name of Jesus.
- Cauldron of witchcraft cooking my flesh, die, in the name of Jesus.
- Let the fire of God kill bewitched cells in my body, in the name of Jesus.
- Blood of Jesus, move upon every area of my life.
- I dismantle every hand of witchcraft, in the name of Jesus.

17. Thou power of cancer, die, in the name of Jesus.
18. Every threat to my life, my God shall threaten you to death, in the name of Jesus.
19. Holy Ghost, break the yoke of cancer in my life, in the name of Jesus.
20. Every devastating attack on my beauty through the attack on my breast, die, in the name of Jesus.
21. Every power behind unprofitable growth, die, in the name of Jesus.
22. Every cancer initiation beginning from the duct in my breast, die, in the name of Jesus.
23. The spirit of cancer, loose your hold and die, in the name of Jesus.
24. You cancer of any kind, i am not your candidate, therefore, leave me alone, in the name of Jesus.

25. Cancer of___, I command you to dry up and die, in the name of Jesus.
26. Every power jingling the bell of untimely death on my life, you, your bell and pronouncements, die, in the name of Jesus.
27. I curse every cancerous cell to die, in the name of Jesus.
28. Every disease of Egypt, i am not your candidate, in the name of Jesus.
29. You demon of unprofitable growth and cell multiplication, i bind you and cast you out, in the name of Jesus.
30. Every re-occurrence of breast cancer in my life, die, in the name of Jesus.
31. Father Lord, let Your power move away every mountain of infirmity in my life, in the name of Jesus.
32. Every sign of inflammatory of breast cancer, die, in the name of Jesus.

33. I receive deliverance from every inherited spirit, in the name of Jesus.
34. Every unusual change in size, or shape or colour of my breast, die, in the name of Jesus.
35. Holy Ghost arise and kill every satanic agent in my life, in the name of Jesus.
36. Every satanic discharge from my nipple, dry up to the source, in the name of Jesus.
37. By the power that divided the Red Sea, let every evil growth in my body dry up, in the name of Jesus.
38. Every solid lump or thickening in any area of my body, be melted away by fire, in the name of Jesus.
39. Every circulating serpent in my body, come out by fire, in the name of Jesus.
40. Any stage breast cancer has reached in my life, today, I terminate your advancement and i command a reversal now, in the name of Jesus.
41. I decree that you will not spread to any other part of my body, in the name of Jesus.
42. Let my body reject every handwriting of darkness, in the name of Jesus.
43. There shall be no reinforcement or regrouping of any cancer attack against me anymore, in the name of Jesus.
44. Let the arrow of darkness release my blood and my organs, in the name of Jesus.
45. Satan, hear me and hear me very well: I am not a death carrier but a life carrier, in the name of Jesus.
46. I speak destruction unto every cancerous cell, in the name of Jesus.

47. Blood of Jesus, mop up all the poison of cancer, in the name of Jesus.
48. Every arrow of cancer, come out now, in the name of Jesus.
49. Every power battling my health, receive the fire of God, in the name of Jesus.
50. By the power in the stripes of Jesus, i kill every power of cancer, in the name of Jesus.
51. The power of pain, be dissolved by fire, in the name of Jesus.
52. O God, arise and let every enemy of my sound health scatter, in the name of Jesus.
53. O cancer, hear the power of the Lord: I command you to dry up, in the name of Jesus.
54. Poison and insects programmed into my body, come out now, in the name of Jesus.
55. I cancel by fire, the evil instructions given to my body, in the name of Jesus.
56. I receive deliverance from the grip of destructive spirit, in the name of Jesus.
57. Holy Ghost fire and blood of Jesus, destroy every contrary handwriting of infirmity.
58. Thank God for your healing.

Thank God for your divine healing.

1. 20 Marching Orders To Fulfill Your Destiny
2. 30 Prophetic Arrows From Heaven
3. 30 Things The Anointing Can Do For You
4. Abraham's Children in Bondage
5. A-Z of Complete Deliverance
6. Basic Prayer Patterns
7. Be Prepared
8. Bewitchment must Die
9. Biblical Principles of Dream Interpretation
10. Born Great, But Tied Down
11. Breaking Bad Habits
12. Breakthrough Prayers For Business Professionals
13. Bringing Down The Power of God
14. Brokenness
15. Can God Trust You?
16. Command The Morning
17. Connecting to The God of Breakthroughs
18. Consecration Commitment & Loyalty
19. Contending For The Kingdom
20. Criminals In The House Of God
21. Dancers At The Gate of Death
22. Dealing Destiny Vultures
23. Dealing With Destiny Thieves
24. Dealing With Hidden Curses
25. Dealing With Local Satanic Technology
26. Dealing With Satanic Exchange
27. Dealing With The Evil Powers Of Your Father's House
28. Dealing With Tropical Demons
29. Dealing With Unprofitable Roots
30. Dealing With Witchcraft Barbers
31. Deep Secrets, Deep Deliverance

32. Deliverance By Fire
33. Deliverance From Evil Foundation
34. Deliverance From Spirit Husband And Spirit Wife
35. Deliverance From The Limiting Powers
36. Deliverance of The Brain
37. Deliverance Of The Conscience
38. Deliverance Of The Head
39. Deliverance of The Tongue
40. Deliverance: God's Medicine Bottle
41. Destiny Clinic
42. Destroying Satanic Masks
43. Disgracing Soul Hunters
44. Divine Military Training
45. Divine Prescription For Your Total Immunity
46. Divine Yellow Card
47. Dominion Prosperity
48. Drawers Of Power From The Heavenlies
49. Evil Appetite
50. Evil Umbrella
51. Facing Both Ways
52. Failure In The School Of Prayer
53. Fire For Life's Journey
54. For We Wrestle ...
55. Freedom Indeed
56. God's Key To A Happy Life
57. Healing Through Prayers
58. Holiness Unto The Lord
59. Holy Cry
60. Holy Fever
61. Hour Of Decision

62. How To Obtain Personal Deliverance
63. How To Pray When Surrounded By The Enemies
64. I Am Moving Forward
65. Idols Of The Heart
66. Igniting Your Inner Fire
67. Is This What They Died For?
68. Kill Your Goliath By Fire
69. Killing The Serpent of Frustration
70. Let Fire Fall
71. Let God Answer By Fire
72. Limiting God
73. Lord, Behold Their Threatening
74. Madness of The Heart
75. Making Your Way Through The Traffic Jam of Life
76. Meat For Champions
77. Medicine For Winners
78. My Burden For The Church
79. Open Heavens Through Holy Disturbance
80. Overpowering Witchcraft
81. Paralysing The Riders And The Horse
82. Personal Spiritual Check-Up
83. Possessing The Tongue of Fire
84. Power Against Coffin Spirits
85. Power Against Destiny Quenchers
86. Power Against Dream Criminals
87. Power Against Local Wickedness
88. Power Against Marine Spirits
89. Power Against Spiritual Terrorists
90. Power Against The Mystery of Wickedness
91. Power Against Unclean Spirits
92. Power Must Change Hands
93. Power of Brokenness

94. Power To Disgrace The Oppressors
95. Power To Recover Your Birthright
96. Power To Recover Your Lost Glory
97. Power To Shut Satanic Doors
98. Pray Your Way To Breakthroughs
99. Prayer Strategies For Singles
100. Prayer Is The Battle
101. Prayer Rain
102. Prayer To Kill Enchantment
103. Prayer To Make You Fulfill Your Divine Destiny
104. Prayer Warfare Against 70 Mad Spirits
105. Prayers For Open Heavens
106. Prayers To Destroy Diseases And Infirmities
107. Prayers To Move From Minimum To Maximum
108. Praying Against Foundational Poverty
109. Praying Against The Spirit Of The Valley
110. Praying In The Storm
111. Praying To Destroy Satanic Roadblocks
112. Praying To Dismantle Witchcraft
113. Principles of Conclusive Prayers
114. Principles Of Prayer
115. Raiding The House of The Strongman
116. Release From Destructive Covenants
117. Revoking Evil Decrees
118. Safeguarding Your Home
119. Satanic Diversion Of The Black Race
120. Secrets of Spiritual Growth And Maturity
121. Setting The Covens Ablaze
122. Seventy Rules of Spiritual Warfare
123. Seventy Sermons To Preach To Your Destiny
124. Silencing The Birds Of Darkness

125. Slave Masters
126. Slaves Who Love Their Chains
127. Smite The Enemy And He Will Flee
128. Speaking Destruction Unto The Dark Rivers
129. Spiritual Education
130. Spiritual Growth And Maturity
131. Spiritual Warfare And The Home
132. Stop Them Before They Stop You
133. Strategic Praying
134. Strategy Of Warfare Praying
135. Students In The School Of Fear
136. Symptoms Of Witchcraft Attack
137. Taking The Battle To The Enemy's Gate
138. The Amazing Power of Faith
139. The Baptism of Fire
140. The Battle Against The Spirit Of Impossibility
141. The Chain Breaker
142. The Dinning Table Of Darkness
143. The Enemy Has Done This
144. The Evil Cry Of Your Family Idol
145. The Fire Of Revival
146. The Gateway To Spiritual Power
147. The Great Deliverance
148. The Hidden Viper
149. The Internal Stumbling Block
150. The Lord is A Man of War
151. The Mystery Of Mobile Curses
152. The Mystery Of The Mobile Temple
153. The Power of Aggressive Prayer Warriors
154. The Power of Priority
155. The Prayer Eagle

156. The Pursuit Of Success
157. The Scale of The Almighty
158. The School of Tribulation
159. The Seasons Of Life
160. The Secrets Of Greatness
161. The Serpentine Enemies
162. The Skeleton In Your Grandfather's Cupboard
163. The Slow Learners
164. The Snake In The Power House
165. The Spirit Of The Crab
166. The Star Hunters
167. The Star In Your Sky
168. The Terrible Agenda
169. The Tongue Trap
170. The Unconquerable Power
171. The University of Champions
172. The Unlimited God
173. The Vagabond Spirit
174. The Way Of Divine Encounter
175. The Wealth Transfer Agenda
176. Tied Down In The Spirits
177. Too Hot To Handle
178. Turnaround Breakthrough
179. Unprofitable Foundations
180. Victory Over Satanic Dreams
181. Victory Over Your Greatest Enemies
182. Violent Prayers Against Stubborn Situations
183. War At The Edge Of Breakthroughs
184. Wasted At The Market Square of Life
185. Wasting The Wasters
186. Wealth Must Change Hands

187. What You Must Know About The House Fellowship
188. When God Is Silent
189. When The Battle is from Home
190. When The Deliverer Need Deliverance
191. When The Enemy Hides
192. When Things Get Hard
193. When You Are Knocked Down
194. When You Are Under Attack
195. When You Need A Change
196. Where Is Your Faith?
197. While Men Slept
198. Woman! Thou Art Loosed.
199. Your Battle And Your Strategy
200. Your Foundation And Destiny
201. Your Mouth And Your Deliverance
202. Your Mouth And Your Warfare

YORUBA PUBLICATIONS

1. Adura Agbayori
2. Adura Ti Nsi Oke Ni' di
3. Ojo Adura

FRENCH PUBLICATIONS

1. Bilan Spirituel Personnel
2. Cantique Des Contiques
3. Commander Le Matin
4. Comment Recevior La Delivrance Du Mari Et Femme De Nuit
5. Cpmment Se Delivrer Soi-meme

6. Demanteler La Sorcellerie
7. En Finir Avec Les Forces Malefiques De La Maison De Ton Pere
8. Espirit De Vagabondage
9. Femme Tu Es Liberee
10. Frappez l'adversaire Et Il Fuira
11. L'etoile Dans Votre Ciel
12. La Deliverance De La Tete
13. La Deliverance: Le Flacon De Medicament Dieu
14. La Deviation Satanique De La Race Noire
15. Le Combat Spirituel Et Le Foyer
16. Le Mauvais Cri Des Idoles
17. Le Programme De Tranfert De Richesse
18. Les Etudiants A l'ecole De La Peur
19. Les Saisons De La Vie
20. Les Strategies De Prieres Pour Les Celibataires
21. Ne Grand Mais Lie
22. Pluie De Priere
23. Pouvoir Contre Les Demond Tropicaux
24. Povoir Contre Les Terrorites Spirituel
25. Prier Jusqu'a Remporter La Victoire
26. Priere De Percees Pour Les Hommes D'affaires
27. Priere Pour Detruire Les Maladies Et Infirmites
28. Prieres Violentes Pour Humilier Les Problemes Opiniatres
29. Prieres De Comat Contre 70 Espirits Dechanines
30. Quand Les Choses Deviennent Difficiles
31. Que l'envoutement Perisse
32. Revoquer Les Decrets Malefiques
33. Se Liberer Des Alliances Malefiques
34. Ton Combat Et Ta Strategie
35. Victoires Sur Les Reves Sataniques
36. Votre Fondement Et Votre Destin

ANNUAL 70 DAYS
PRAYER AND FASTING PUBLICATIONS

1. Prayers That Bring Miracles
2. Let God Answer By Fire
3. Prayers To Mount With Wings As Eagles
4. Prayers That Bring Explosive Increase
5. Prayers For Open Heavens
6. Prayers To Make You Fulfill Your Divine Destiny
7. Prayers That Make God To Answer And Fight By Fire
8. Prayers That Bring Unchallengeable Victory And Breakthrough Rainfall Bombardments
9. Prayers That Bring Dominion Prosperity And Uncommon Success
10. Prayers That Bring Power And Overflowing Progress
11. Prayers That Bring Laughter And Enlargement Breakthroughs
12. Prayers That Bring Uncommon Favour And Breakthroughs
13. Prayers That Bring Unprecedented Greatness And Unmatchable Increase
14. Prayers That Bring Awesome Testimonies And Turn Around Breakthroughs
15. Prayers That Bring Glorious Restoration
16. Prayers That Bring Unrivaled Lifting

1. Daughters of Philip
2. I Decree An Uncommon Change
3. Power To Fulfil Your Destiny
4. Principles of A Successful Marriage
5. The Call of God
6. When Your Destiny Is Under Attack
7. Woman of Wonder
8. Violence Against Negative Voices

The Books, Tapes and CDs (Audio and Video) All Obtainable At:

- **MFM International Bookshop**
  13, Olasimbo Street, Onike, Yaba, Lagos
- **MFM Prayer City**
  Km 12, Lagos/Ibadan Expressway
- **Battle Cry Christian Ministries**
  322, Herbert Macaulay Way, Sabo, Yaba, Lagos
  Phone: 01 8044415, 0803 304 4239
- **54, Akeju Street, off Shipeolu Street**
  Palmgrove, Lagos
- **All MFM Churches Nationwide**
- **All Leading Christian Bookstores**
- **Battle Cry Christian Ministries**
  Abuja Zonal Office & Bookshop
  No 4, Nasarawa Street, Block A,
  Shop 4, Garki Old Market.
  Phone: 08135865868, 08159103039.